Lighten Your Backpack

Copyright © 2015 Mark Landers

All rights reserved.

ISBN-10: 1518659012
ISBN-13: 978-1518659010

Lighten Your Backpack

How to Simplify Life In a Complex World

Mark R. Landers

This book is dedicated to my grandfather, Ken Landers. You lived a simple and enjoyable life that was true to the Canadian dream. Thanks for your great example and all the great things that you brought to this world.

Contents

Introduction 1

Chapter 1 7
Success in Life is about Progress, Not Perfection

Chapter 2 11
Eliminate Clutter and Feel Energized

Chapter 3 15
Feel Good about Saying No

Chapter 4 21
Understand your Strengths and Focus on them

Chapter 5 27
Optimize your Productivity and Take More Time off

Chapter 6 33
Your Best Investment: Relationships

Chapter 7 37
A Savings Secret: Pay yourself First

Chapter 8 43
The Power of Time, Compound Interest, and Tax Free Investing

Chapter 9 47
Understand your Insurance Coverage and Sleep Better at Night

Chapter 10 53
Your Vision for the Life You Want to Live

Final Thoughts 59

The Simple Plan Program 63

Connect with Us 66

Introduction

Do you feel like you're walking around with a giant backpack weighing you down all the time? How heavy is it—and does it seem like it's getting heavier as you go through life and become more burdened with complications?

My metaphorical backpack has been very heavy at different points in my life. My 20's were a period when I experienced a great deal of growth in my life. Between my desire to start a business, be a good husband, have a successful financial future, fulfill my parents' dreams for me, and keep my health in check, my backpack was super heavy!

The crazy thing was, I did not even realize how much weight I had on my shoulders. I just thought this was normal for life as an adult. Things were complicated, I had very little time, and I was rarely enjoying the things I really valued. Instead, I spent a great deal of time doing the things I thought I should be doing. And so I was constantly feeling frustrated, unaccomplished, and trapped in a life that was too complex and gave me little time to focus on what was really important to me. This is something I now call The Complex Life Trap™.

From the outside, things looked great. I was newly married, had a beautiful home, a growing business, lots of hobbies, and many caring friends and family. I even had a cute little red sports car to enjoy on the weekends. People who knew me would comment on how I was doing all the right things and that I was going to be really successful. Some even wondered why I was in such a hurry to get so much done. One of my early mentors once said that I was 26 years old going on 40.

I tried to enjoy the great compliments and all my accomplishments. But despite all the positive feedback about my current and future success, nothing ever seemed to be enough. I continued to strive for more accomplishments, more possessions, more recognition, and all the other markers of success I felt I should have.

A turning point

Then on December 9, 2010, my life took a significant turn. Only a month after moving into a big, beautiful new home (another one of my visions in pursuit of success), my wife and I had an extremely intense conversation. We talked about our feelings, goals, and future. It seemed that our paths had gone in different directions. And it felt like these paths were now too far apart. I believe my wife still wanted what we had planned out in our early 20's, but I had lost that picture. I was so focused on my pursuit of success and money, I had neglected to focus on our relationship. We decided it would be best if we separated.

I remember this day in December very vividly. I packed up my car with my essential belongings and moved out of the house, driving over to my "new" home. It was a terrible drive with lots of emotion. I had many thoughts about whether I was doing the right thing. After about an hour in the car, I arrived at an old faithful spot to rest my head, my childhood home in Mississauga, Ontario. Yes, I was going to stay at my parent's place. I brought my things in, and I shared my emotions with my Mom and Dad. They were in shock about the whole situation, but assured me that all would be OK. And there I was, lodged in my old bedroom in the basement! I recall going to sleep that night thinking...I just left a 3,000 sq. ft. detached home for an 8 x 11 room in my parents' basement - what have I done?

Still, despite the immense emotions connected to the end of a marriage, I did feel a sense of excitement, as there was a whole new world of possibilities opening up to me.

Simplify and live better

I think many people face the same challenges I did. There is so much complexity in today's society. Things seem to change at a rate no one can keep up with. We seem to work longer hours than ever before, our smartphones never stop ringing and pinging, and there seems to be so little time to focus on our health. We have even less time for our families and less money to save for the future.

To help people like you focus on what's important and simplify your life, we have developed a series of basic tips that we enjoy sharing. So far, we have had great success helping people apply the tips in their lives and progress through our program. It is very rewarding to see people take steps to focus on what is important in their lives.

This book gives you a high-level summary of the 10 steps so you can get started thinking about how you might apply them. For a deeper understanding, please visit this book's website: **www.LightenYourBackpack.com**.

Chapter 1

Success in Life is about Progress, Not Perfection

Like me, you've no doubt noticed that life seems to be getting more complicated. Between work, kids, trying to stay fit, looking after aging parents, taking care of the house, and trying to save a bit of money, it's not an easy battle! Many people have dreams of creating a "simpler life," but most are not even sure where to begin.

I feel very fortunate to have participated in Dan Sullivan's amazing *Strategic Coach Program*. He developed this program to assist entrepreneurs in building self-managing companies. Through participating in these sessions, I have experienced a number of breakthroughs - one occurred after I read Dan's book, *Learning How to Avoid the Gap*. This book explains the underlying strategy for building lifetime happiness by using a unique way to measure progress through life.

As we go through life, we're constantly measuring and assessing ourselves on a variety of factors: physical appearance, wealth, intelligence, relationships, and possessions. We have a vision or an ideal about what life would be like if we could improve in any of these areas. Personally, I have fought with my weight for a number of years and often think about how I would feel at the perfect weight. These visions of the ideal are often the inspiration for goals. In my case, the goal is to eat healthier and exercise more. The excitement then begins!

Action plan

Significant goals take time to achieve. When setting them, most of us start with a review of our current situation. We then figure out what our target is and what success looks like. We begin moving forward with an action plan and start making progress. But we typically hit a few road blocks, and our progress slows down.

This is often the point where we review how we've done, comparing our progress to the goals we've set. In my personal example, let's say my goal is to drop from 220 to 200 pounds. I'm one month into my new, healthier regime and I've lost four pounds. Only 16 more to go! I then begin thinking about how tough it was to lose the first four pounds. How am I going to be able to go through this ordeal for another six months? What about my upcoming vacation? How am I going to stay on track at an all-inclusive resort?

The inner dialogue goes on and on. This often leads to unhappiness and a lack of confidence, and may result in abandonment of the goal itself. Dan Sullivan calls this type of thinking "getting stuck in the gap."

A different approach

If we take a different approach to measurement, we can often change the way we feel about progress, and build more self-confidence.

Let's say I focus all my progress measurement against my starting point. I know that getting to 200 pounds (loss of 20) is my end goal, but I'm going to try to forget about that for a moment. My starting point was 220 and now I'm at 216. This is something to be celebrated! I'm going to think about all the eating habits I changed to get there, and how many times I exercised in the last month.

This method of measurement is much more fulfilling. It helps build more confidence and is much more likely to keep you focused on the eventual achievement of your end goal.

Measure from your starting point

Throughout life we will set thousands of goals, some as small as getting to work on time, and others as significant as paying off our mortgage or having enough money to retire comfortably.

The sooner you begin measuring progress from your starting point versus the end result, the sooner you will begin building confidence and feel happier about your life.

Chapter 2

Eliminate Clutter and Feel Energized

The accumulation of "stuff" or "clutter" happens gradually over the course of a lifetime. At various stages in life we buy, collect, and receive thousands of items, some of which we continue to use or keep around for practical or aesthetic value and some of which we have no real need of. And many of these items we could part with quite easily. A quick look at the end of your driveway on garbage day confirms that!

There are other items that, despite their lack of use, never seem to make it to the curb. You may think you will use this item later, it may have sentimental value, or perhaps you spent a pile of hard-earned money on it. We have all had those conversations with ourselves (or perhaps more often with our spouse)! The reality is, many of these items we never really needed, and our brains have a very tough time coming to terms with that fact. The stronger the emotional or financial connection to the item, the greater likelihood that you will keep it around.

Negative emotions

Mess or clutter created by the accumulation of unused items can be a real distraction. When we have an overwhelming amount of items and they are misplaced or ignored, many different negative emotions typically surface. Feelings of frustration, anger, and unproductiveness often eat away at us, causing us to miss deadlines and feel unaccomplished and stressed out - which can lead to a very unhappy life.

Like many great things in life, the decision to declutter is one that will throw many entrepreneurs into a place outside of their comfort zone. The decision to part with those clothes that don't fit any more (size or style), those Visa bills from 1996, or those hockey sticks your kids used in Novice 20 years ago is not easy. Your impeccable filing system, the memories of that awesome night in Miami in that trendy designer outfit, and your first set of golf clubs all invoke wonderful memories. But by clearing out these items and creating space in your life, you will attract new things, new systems of organizing, and new experiences. These new parts of your life can only happen if there is room to accept them.

The buffet of life

Let's use a real-life scenario to illustrate. Imagine it's your Mom's birthday. She decides she would like the family to go to a buffet Chinese restaurant to celebrate. You get inside, secure a table, and then make your way up to the buffet. You grab a plate and then begin putting together a well-rounded meal. Your plate is now full, you are just about to walk to your table, and you notice the chef bringing out a fresh platter of teriyaki chicken. You would love to load up on it, but your plate is already full. By the time you finish your plate and get back to the buffet for round 2, the chicken is gone and you have missed out.

Life is no different; if you are completely consumed with all the things you already have, your mind will not allow room for new items, opportunities, and experiences. Besides clearing space, eliminating clutter will also clear your mind for exciting possibilities in the future.

Start small

A simple approach to getting the ball rolling is to start with a small goal and gradually work toward larger projects. Start with decluttering a drawer or a cabinet, and enjoy the feeling of accomplishment after the work is done. Then you can gradually gear up to tackling that cluttered garage or basement.

With this approach, you will be on the right track to eliminating clutter from your life. This process will energize you, make you feel more confident, and ensure you have a secure feeling of control. You will be able to think clearly, make better decisions, and live an overall happier life. Why not start today?

Chapter 3

Feel Good about Saying No

Athletes spend a lot of time stretching and extending their bodies. But over-extending can cause injury. It's the same outside of the athletic arena: We can stretch ourselves and discover new ways to feel fulfilled and make our dreams come true. But we have to be careful not to over-extend ourselves.

The truth is that half of the troubles in life can be traced to saying yes too quickly and not saying no soon enough. We rush in impulsively without considering the consequences to our own health and wellbeing.

In Canada where we live the good life, so many of us are stressed from being overcommitted and pulled in a million different directions. It's shocking how stress sabotages health. Scientists tell us that around 50 per cent of all serious illness is directly caused by stress. It's been called the scourge of the century.

What are you getting yourself into?

Think about those situations - even people - that drag you down and "zap" your energy. You may be exhausted but still say yes to extra volunteer work, working overtime to help out colleagues, attending social events, or doing favours for friends. Or what about that needy colleague who backs you into a corner and monologues about their personal problems while your work sits unfinished? Your impulse may be to run away but you allow yourself to become drained by their bad energy.

These are all ways you may let your good nature overtake the need to look after yourself. All your efforts may not even be appreciated, and the result is that you feel even more tired and run-down—which makes you vulnerable to insomnia, colds and flu, and other stress reactions.

Saying no is a skill

For us people pleasers, it's a real challenge to draw the line and say no. And yet we need to make our own happiness the top priority and try our best to leave the guilt behind.

Just remember, saying no doesn't make you a bad person. It doesn't make you insensitive. Rather, it means you are strong and confident with your boundaries and limits.

Practice saying "no" in front of the mirror, and smile when you're saying it. You can actually learn to feel good about saying no, instead of guilt-ridden.

Your YES and NO list

A super-simple method for learning to say no is to make a **YES and NO list**. Jot down all the things you love doing, things you are passionate about, and things that give you energy. This is your **YES** list.

Then make a list of things you dislike doing, things that frustrate you and drain your energy. This is your **NO** list.

You can then use these lists as tools to help you make decisions. If it's in the NO list, it's probably something you should avoid. If it's in the YES list, it will likely enhance your life.

The awesome thing is that there are probably many people in this world who have a lot of the items on your NO list at the very top of their YES list. Your YES and NO list enables you to figure out people's strengths and work together to assign roles on projects. This can be great at the office, around the house, and in community organizations.

You hate coaching kids' soccer games? Your friend down the street loves it, but has no desire to lead adult hiking trips on Sundays - something you really like doing.

Try it out and see what happens. You might be surprised by the insights you arrive at.

Chapter 4

Understand your Strengths and Focus on them

Early in life we discover we are great at some things, OK at other things, and not so great at many things. But our tendency is to try to become great at the things we are weak at. We work hard, and tough it out, all in an effort to get better.

Of course, it's always good to try to improve ourselves and become more proficient. But for those things we've always been weak at, we may be wasting our efforts. That's because there are only a few things we do on this planet that excite us, engage us and provide us with enough energy to keep doing them for hours on end. Conversely, there are many things in life that drag us down and can frustrate us in mere minutes.

The trick is to focus on our strengths and delegate tasks we are weak at. This way, we can make the best use of our time and energy.

The challenges of delegating

Delegating may seem difficult at first. Many people feel guilty about it. Or we are worried that no one can complete the delegated tasks as well as ourselves. It can be hard to let go and trust people you delegate to. But it's not good for your health to try to do everything.

A more optimum situation is to recognize that there are likely many people on Earth who are just amazing at tasks that you or I have no natural aptitude for.

Thus, the ultimate, most effective team is comprised of people with complementary strengths and weaknesses who can work well together.

Take the Kolbe test

A great tool to understand your natural strengths is the Kolbe A Index. You can take this by visiting: **www.kolbe.com**.

Try taking the Kolbe A index for insight into how you naturally initiate when solving problems. Ask your team members to take the test as well. Or even your spouse. The results will amaze you. It was such a breakthrough when I received my results. It really gave great context to many of my reactions to past experiences in life. The test results can also help you best leverage working with your team so that everyone is focusing on their strengths and not spinning their wheels trying to get better at their weaknesses.

The optimum team

You might then have to make some adjustments. For instance, a five-person team of big-idea people with no aptitude for the small details may not be very effective. If you want to come up with ideas and have other people execute them, you need to surround yourself with people who can best complement the areas that you are not as naturally good at.

According to Dan Sullivan, founder of The Strategic Coach, everyone has one Unique Ability that no one else has. He defines it as "a superior ability that other people notice and value; second, we love doing it and want to do it as much as possible; third, it is energizing both for us and others around us; and, fourth, we keep getting better, never running out of possibilities for further improvement."

You may want to block off some time to sit down and make a list of the things you are really good at, and which you are better at than anyone you know. From that introspection, you can gradually understand what you should be focusing on, and what you need to delegate to people around you.

As Dan Sullivan says, it's all about guarding your time and prioritizing: "You need to protect your time and attention, reserving it just for those decisions, relationships, and opportunities that need your particular skills and wisdom. If you don't do this, your business (or life) will be limited to what you, personally, can do on any given day. But .... develop a team whose abilities complement your own, and you'll suddenly find yourself with more time...."

Chapter 5

Optimize your Productivity and Take More Time off

There are two ways to tackle a long-distance hike. You can do it as fast as possible, going all out every day, blasting along the trail without stopping until the end of each long day, and dropping into bed exhausted.

Or, you can take more time, perhaps a couple of extra days, and build regular breaks into the schedule so you can enjoy the scenery, eat, rest, and refresh yourself. The whole experience will be more fun and memorable.

Life is like this too, especially when it comes to how much time we spend working to exhaustion versus taking time off to recover and rejuvenate.

For most of us, we are typically told at a young age that to be most successful in our careers, we must work harder than everyone else. It's drilled into us that the "time and effort" we expend will eventually be rewarded with income and status.

Over the last 20 years, however, our professions have shifted to a model where we are rewarded more for the results of our work—and less for the "time and effort" we put into it.

The challenge of shifting gears

Shifting into this different gear can be challenging if we are used to thinking that the harder and longer we work, the more we'll be rewarded. With work styles built around long hours, doing everything ourselves, and that feeling of accomplishment after a 12 or 14-hour day or working over the weekend, we end up focusing more on the number of hours we work than on the quality of our work. It's easy to fall into the trap of feeling like a hero because we work so many hours.

Overtime and overwork, though, can often result in a decline in the quality of work and the ability to maintain focus. It also takes time away from other important parts of life such as our health, family, friends, and personal interests.

Anthropologists have long noted that tribal people in remote parts of the world have much more leisure time than modern Western working people like ourselves. They work hard in short bursts, but they also spend a lot of time just hanging out talking, laughing, playing with the kids, and feasting. Their verbal communication skills are often extremely well honed because they talk to each other face to face so much.

We can definitely take a page from these more relaxed lifestyles.

Keep results in the forefront

To be most efficient and effective, we need to keep "results" in the forefront, employing delegation and teamwork, and keeping ourselves extremely sharp.

One of the best ways to stay sharp is to schedule a sufficient amount of time away from work to look after all the other "stuff" in our lives. That includes staying healthy through exercise and diet, and visiting our doctor regularly for check-ups.

And it means spending time with our partner, children, family and friends; pursuing our most important personal goals and hobbies - and of course spending time relaxing!

Personally, after a great long weekend, or an excellent family trip, I usually come back to work refreshed and full of energy and creative ideas.

Build vacation days into your calendar

It takes some planning to ensure we have free time away from work. As a starting point, grab a 12-month calendar, and talk to your partner about what dates are ideal to book as time off from work. Try to block off at least a few vacation days every quarter.

And the final point: guard those days off like a hawk! It's okay to exchange your planned vacation days for other dates if things come up - just don't cancel them.

Next time you are feeling stressed and overworked, or it seems like nothing in your life is making sense, try taking a day off work. Plan that day for yourself, and see how much better the time off makes you feel!

Chapter 6

Your Best Investment: Relationships

What makes you feel more excited: anticipating dinner with your best friend, or finally getting that new smartphone app you've heard so much about?

Technology is a powerful tool, and you can either use it to keep your distance from other people or facilitate stronger connections with them. It should never be subservient to the relationships you foster with friends, family, business associates, and clients—even though we're all constantly bombarded with new ways to electronically communicate: email, text message, Facebook, instant message, Facetime, Skype, and probably many more in the near future.

These easy means of communication are often utilized in place of personal, one-on-one contact. So we are increasingly forging more fleeting electronic relationships and fewer genuine personal relationships—which can lead to a sense of social isolation.

E-confusion

Have you ever used electronic communication to avoid an in-person confrontation? It seems like a good idea in theory, as we can spend time rewriting and editing our point of view before we send the message.

But many times these written messages just lead to confusion, as the written words are unable to convey emotions and thoughts as accurately as talking in person, face to face. It's so easy to press "send" or "post," but the ensuing confusion is often more difficult to deal with than looking someone in the eye and discussing things carefully. It takes more sophisticated interpersonal skills to deal with an issue in person, but these skills are definitely worth learning and building on. Of course, many companies, sectors and industries have relocated to other parts of the world, which means you have to work harder at communicating effectively with colleagues on different continents.

The best plan is to take advantage of the efficiency and speed of electronic communication, while always choosing the best way to craft the content of your message.

Outmoded systems

Many people feel that to thrive in today's business world, they need to become expert at the next great piece of technology - such as a new purchase order system or a new accounting system. Then by the time they've mastered it, a new system has come along, or the system is updated and they're back to the drawing board learning something new. Sometimes these new systems become so robust they end up replacing employees or entire businesses. Therefore, if we can position ourselves in business ventures and careers that are mainly focused on interacting with people, creating value, and creative thinking, we will have a lot more longevity than if we specialize in a specific system.

Relationships always in style

No matter what direction technology takes, people and businesses will always have challenges and problems to solve. As Dan Sullivan says, "Micro technology, no matter how fast and powerful, will never replace two uniquely human capabilities: the ability to create an infinite number of new things, and the ability to relate to other human beings in an infinite number of new ways."

To be well positioned for growth, align your career and business opportunities with this approach. Take the best of technology and use it to your advantage for its greatest features. Just remember that your most valuable investment is in relationships. They never seem to fall out of style!

Chapter 7

A Savings Secret: Pay yourself First

It's fun to spend money, and, as one of the core principles of economics states, human beings have unlimited wants. So the big challenge in life is maintaining a balance between saving for things you want to buy in the future, and spending on things today.

As certain reality TV shows reveal, most people are really good at spending but not very good at saving. Their approach to finances and budgets is to set a goal that, as of next month, they are going to begin to spend less and save more for the future.

The first of the month rolls around, and they begin to keep an eye on their bank account. They see their bill payments come out, and they commit to taking whatever funds are left over at the end of the month and allocating those toward their retirement plan. Throughout the month, they try to watch their expenses, but amazingly, by the 30th they are only able to get the bills paid.

The net result is no additional funds for savings. They then set the same goal for next month, and the cycle repeats. A few months later, they feel really frustrated that they are making little progress. So, in an effort to feel better, they invest in some "retail therapy" and enjoy a weekend shopping spree on their credit card! They then struggle over the next few months and scrape by to pay it off. The net result is an overall feeling of frustration and no progress toward their savings goal.

Pay yourself at the start of the month

A simple solution, instead of trying to "pay yourself last" at the end of the month with whatever is left over, is to "pay yourself first" at the beginning of the month - before everyone else gets their hands on your cash. This means having money automatically routed at the beginning of the month to a designated savings vehicle. If you can allocate a percentage of your income into savings this way, it will shock you to see how you can still get your bills paid every month despite having a bit less money to do so. Setting up payments to be automatic is the key!

This can be done in a number of ways:

1. Automatic transfers from your chequing account to savings or extra payments to credit cards, through online banking or telephone banking.

2. Pre-authorized withdrawal programs with investment or retirement savings providers.

3. Extra mortgage payments by contacting your mortgage provider and requesting they increase your regular payments (even $100 monthly can make a big difference over time).

4. Employer sponsored savings plans. This one is really easy; your employer withholds a portion of your paycheque and directs it towards a savings plan before it hits your bank account.

The great thing about many of these automatic savings vehicles is that they are flexible and can be increased or decreased any time. So if you receive a bonus at work, adjust your transfer to be a bit extra for a couple of months. Or if your car breaks down this month, turn off your savings plan and restart it a few months later.

How much to save

Everyone wonders what the "magic number" to save every year is or "How much do I need invested to retire?" This is truly an individual question, as there are so many different scenarios and goals. For advice tailored to your own circumstances, speak to a qualified financial planner.

A rule of thumb I typically use with my clients is to save 10-20% of your income every month. For me personally, this is what I strive to do....some months more successfully than others. Of course, 20% is a fairly large percentage if you are not accustomed to this type of investing. It's no different than exercise......if you are not habituated to regular exercise it's tough to jump off the couch and run a marathon. So, start nice, easy and small: possibly 3% or 5% of your income. Set a goal to increase by 1 or 2% every few months. A few years later you'll look back and have a nice chunk of cash set aside! Remember, every little bit counts.

Chapter 8

The Power of Time, Compound Interest, and Tax Free Investing

Does investing seem difficult and challenging to you? If your goal is to save enough money to retire comfortably without ever running out of money, you are likely exclusively focused on how to get the best rate of return on your investments. You may meet with a number of advisors at various financial institutions, attend seminars, and read articles in magazines and on the Internet. You may even obsessively research a "hot tip" a friend shared with you after a few cocktails at a dinner party.

The result may be an unstructured approach, duplication of effort, overwhelming complexity, high stress, and uncertainty about being able to meet your basic financial needs in retirement. This lack of confidence may hold you back from pursuing some of the things you really want in life!

But building an investment plan based exclusively on high rates of return is only one piece of the puzzle. There are three other pieces, including:

- The amount of time money is invested
- The effects of compound interest
- The rate of taxes paid on various investments

A simple example with a toonie

Let's say you decided to invest just a toonie (a CA$2 coin, for those of you south of the border). Let's also suggest you could find a fantastic investment that would enable you to double this $2 every year for 20 years. So, after one year you'd have $4; after two years, $8; after three years, $16. This growth on top of growth is the compound interest.

Now, let's also include a rate of tax. In Canada the top tax rate is about 46%, so that's what we will use for our example. Can you guess how much this investment would be worth after 20 years? The answer is **$10,673**. Not bad for 2 bucks, eh?

How going tax-free makes a big difference

Here is a super-interesting spin on this example. Let's say we find an investment vehicle that enables the money to grow on a tax-free basis. In Canada, we have an awesome opportunity called the Tax Free Savings Account (TFSA), created by the Canadian government in 2009. You can invest money, allow it to grow tax-free, and eventually withdraw it tax-free! Similar opportunities also exist within RRSP accounts, as well as cash-value life insurance.

Adding the tax-free spin to our example, $2, doubling every year for 20 years without any tax, would be worth a whopping **$2,097,152.** The difference is truly amazing!

I will be the first to admit this is a magnified example. There are very few opportunities to invest long term and double your money every year. But this example truly does highlight the impact that taxes can have on investing.

When planning for a comfortable retirement, it is imperative to evaluate investment options beyond just the sticker. The sticker in this case is the rate of return. The impact of this investment on your overall financial plan is really what counts. It goes much deeper than which product to buy. Rather, you need to layer all the right pieces of your plan to ensure a lifetime of financial security.

And remember: The value of developing a proper retirement income plan with ongoing input from an experienced financial planner will go a long way to reduce stress about your retirement. When was the last time you reviewed the funding of your retirement plan? If you are like most, it's been a while! Take a step today to reduce stress and simplify your finances. You'll be very happy that you did!

Chapter 9

Understand your Insurance Coverage and Sleep Better at Night

There are no guarantees in life, but purchasing adequate insurance is one concrete way you can eliminate some of the uncertainty about what would happen to your family or business in the event of job loss, illness, death, or other unforeseen occurrences.

After all, life these days is not as stable as it used to be. Things were different just a few generations ago. People seemed to enjoy much more stability and security with their careers, relationships, and finances. Now things seem to change at a head-spinning pace, causing us to adjust on a yearly basis to what we used to adjust to just once a decade.

That difficult conversation

Unfortunately, most people are reluctant to think, let alone talk, about the possibility of being unable to work because of becoming disabled, or not being able to provide for their families because of death. These are very difficult conversations to have, and the natural inclination is to avoid them and simply hope for the best.

But it's better to take the time now to think through these adverse scenarios and educate yourself about the insurance coverage options available. With confidence gained from learning as much as possible about insurance, you'll be better prepared for the future.

How much coverage do you need?

The starting point for building confidence in your insurance plans is to determine how much coverage you need. Let's use life insurance as an example. In considering your personal situation, here are a few questions that impact the coverage amount: Do you have a mortgage? Do you have an emergency fund? Do you plan to help your kids or grandkids with their education? Or do you have any charitable organizations that you would like to leave funds to?

If you own a business, here are some things that impact coverage amount: Would your company need access to liquid funds for operations? Are there any business debts? Are there any tax liabilities that will be triggered, or is your shareholder agreement properly funded?

By working through questions like these, you will be in the best position to determine the proper amount of coverage to procure. Depending on your circumstances, there may be many more questions to ask; however, the questions above are a great starting point.

What's your current coverage?

The next important step is to take a closer look at the insurance benefits you already have through your workplace, your personal insurance plans, and insurance owned through your mortgage or attached to any associations you belong to. Take some time to understand these products, and you'll feel much better knowing more about the insurance protection you already own. Often the terms and conditions of these policies may be difficult to interpret. A qualified insurance advisor can be a great asset in helping you understand the fine details of the various plans. Similar to many other things in life, the devil is in the details, so make sure you understand them!

Close the gaps in your coverage

Once you've determined the amount of coverage you need and surveyed the insurance products you currently have in place, the next important step is to implement a plan to insure any shortfalls. For instance, you may have purchased insurance a number of years ago, but since then you have purchased a cottage or possibly gotten married again. Or, you may have changed employers and you no longer have disability insurance. These types of life changes can lead to gaps in your coverage. A qualified insurance advisor can be a great asset to assist in helping you secure coverage to close these gaps.

Life is full of opportunities and interests. Why not clear some worry off your plate so you'll be in a better position to take advantage of those opportunities and ultimately sleep a lot better at night?

Free online resources

Get started today by checking out some of the resources online that can help you determine your insurance needs. One excellent resource is at: **www.lifehappens.org**.

Find out what is right for your needs, and give yourself one less thing to worry about in today's ever-changing environment!

Chapter 10

Your Vision for the Life You Want to Live

Business and personal goal setting has become an integral and valuable part of our culture. It's a simple, effective way to plan for the future and get things done. In theory, it should be possible to achieve many diverse goals, just by creating an action plan for each one.

But although it sounds simple, the experience of setting a goal and achieving it often falls off the rails, especially when multiple goals are set. This causes the goal-setter to veer off in a number of different directions at once, leading to confusion and chaos. Some of the goals may be achieved, but the expected feeling of satisfaction may be either less intense and exciting - or completely missing. This spurs the individual to set new goals and repeat the whole process over again.

The missing element

What's missing is an overall vision at the beginning of the process of setting goals, something to strategically tie everything together.

Why are you setting these goals? What are you hoping to get out of them? How do these goals fit with your life and interests? How do you want to feel when they are achieved?

Your vision is the master plan that can guide your goal setting. It helps you clearly understand:

- What you value
- What is important to you
- The most important things you want to accomplish

We have found that clarifying a vision is an important step for the members we have taken through our program. This important step gave them the focus they needed to understand what was really important to them. If you've never actually sat down and thought about this, you'll find it a very enlightening process in which you may uncover things about yourself you had never considered.

After the vision is clarified, goal setting can become much more focused and precise. Goals then tend to build off of each other, with much more satisfying results.

To help you develop your own Simple Life Vision, here is the question we use to start the conversation with our members:

"If your life was totally organized and simple, and you could spend much more time doing the things you really value, what would you be doing, and how would you be feeling?"

For instance, would you be spending more time with your family? Would you have more chances to travel internationally? Or what about that interest you've never been able to cultivate: playing a musical instrument, learning to build a computer, volunteering at a senior's home? Are these the things that would make you happier and/or reduce your stress level?

Take some time and jot down a few thoughts. I think you will be pleased with what you come up with!

The next key important step is to determine the three most important actions you need to take to move forward with your vision. For example: "To spend more time with my family, I need to spend fewer weekends at the office, pay down my debt, and talk to my spouse more about my plans."

If you can take some time to focus on these projects, you will be off to a great start in creating a simpler, more enjoyable life.

Refocusing

When you develop a plan, goals or a vision, life can still throw you some curves and even some knockout punches along the way.

It's no different than a pilot flying from Toronto to the beautiful Hawaiian islands. Once they take off and get the plane up to 30,000 feet, they set the auto pilot. Every so often they need to check in on their course. If winds or weather shift, they adjust the settings and get things back on track to Hawaii.

After developing your vision, keep reviewing it and make small adjustments along the way. At some point you may even need to completely refresh your vision. That's perfectly fine. Just make sure to enjoy every step of the journey!

Final Thoughts

You may be wondering what has happened to me since that night in my parents' basement in 2010. Well, my life has truly moved in a direction I would never have predicted - and yes, I did move out of the basement. I have done so many awesome things that were not in the cards before. From backpacking Southeast Asia, to having an awesome bachelor pad in downtown Toronto, to breaking out and starting my own company, and now training for my first half-marathon, it has been an exciting time. I still keep very busy; however, I have made some significant progress in focusing on the things I want and love to do. It feels great to spend more time doing what I enjoy with people I care about the most.

The key to getting back on track was to focus on simplifying my life – or lightening my backpack. It has been said that "in the beginning you create habits and in the end habits create you." At times it was difficult to shift my habits away from my old thinking. Overall, it has been an extremely rewarding experience and has given me a lot more confidence in the future.

I hope my story and these steps will help guide you and even help you avoid some of the tough times I experienced. Keep in mind that anything you experience is a positive: either the result is favourable and enjoyable, or the result is negative and you are taught lessons in life you will never forget.

A special gift

Simplifying life seems like a great idea; however, many people wonder where to get started. As a special thanks for taking the time to read our book, we would like to offer a special free gift to help you get started.

Please visit this book's website at: **LightenYourBackpack.com** and click on the section marked **Free Gift** to obtain yours now.

The **Simple Plan** Program™

If you are interested in learning more about simplifying your life, we have developed an advanced service called *The Simple Plan Program™*. This is a program where we help successful families create a three-part plan to totally simplify their lives. We also help eliminate *The Complex Life Trap™*.

We created *The Simple Plan Program™* based on our experience working with hundreds of clients and their families. We have learned that many successful families get into trouble because their life is too complicated. Life feels like a treadmill, with no significant progress. They feel stressed and worried. Without a plan in place, their lifestyle could be vulnerable in the event of a sudden change in their situation. Ultimately, they may remain stuck in complexity, and not able to achieve their most important goals.

However, if you take the time to create a plan to simplify your life, you will likely achieve a much better result. You will feel more relaxed and confident. You will be able to make better long-term decisions. You will protect yourself and your family from unexpected events. You will have more time to enjoy yourself. You will feel more fulfilled and empowered, and more likely to achieve your most important goals.

That's why we recommend you do three things:

1. Honestly assess the current complexity in your life.

2. Create a vision for a simpler, more enjoyable life.

3. Develop and implement a three-part plan to achieve your Simple Life Vision.

To help determine if you may be a fit for our program, we have developed a free 90-minute starter session where we help you come up with a vision for a simpler, more enjoyable life and an action plan to achieve it. We can then decide together if you should join the program.

For further information, please visit **www.simpleplanprogram.com** or call 416-705-6640.

Connect with Us!

We would love to hear your story.
Let us know what steps are helping simplify your life!

Join the conversation:

facebook

Simple Plan Program

@SimplePlanMark

Or find Mark on

Linked in

Contact Mark through our website at:

www.LightenYourBackpack.com

Made in the USA
Charleston, SC
23 February 2016